This journal belongs to:

_____

ISBN: 978-1-955418-09-6

Published by The Write Legacy

Interior designed using Canva Pro
Cover art: Miss Celie hand-drawn by Ashley Witcher
Background Elements by Canva Pro

Dear God

Dear God

Dear God

Dear God

Dear God

Dear God

Dear God

Dear God

Dear God

Dear God

Dear God

Dear God

Dear God

Dear God _____

Dear God

Dear God,

Dear God

Dear God

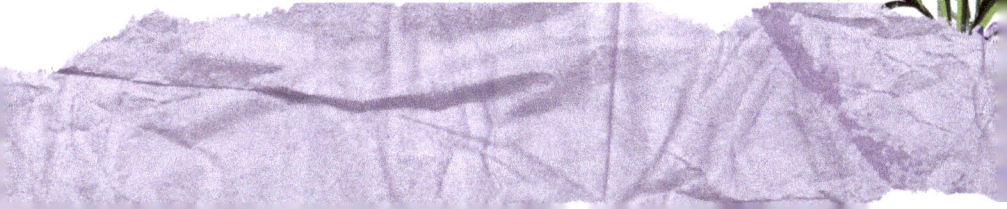

Dear God

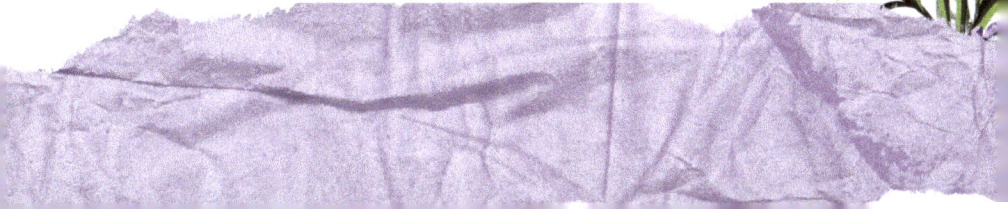

Dear God_____

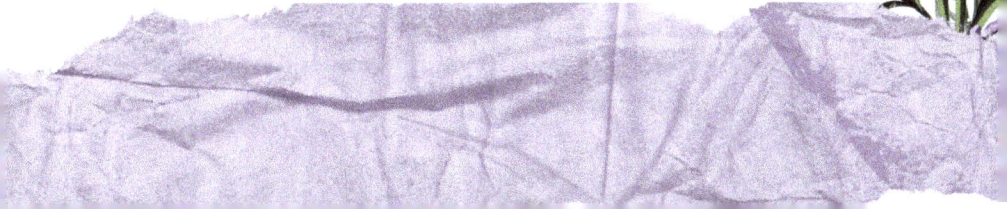

Dear God

Dear God

Dear God

Dear God

Dear God

Dear God

Dear God

Dear God

Dear God

Dear God

Dear God

www.ingramcontent.com/pod-product-compliance
Lightning Source LLC
Chambersburg PA
CBHW071406160426
42813CB00084B/537